Weekly Time Sheet Log Book

Belongs to

Name:

Adress:

Business Adress:

Email:

Mobile Telephone:

Home Telephone:

Fax:

Name:	Month/Year:

Day	Date	Time in	Time out	Breaks	Overtime	Total
Monday						
Tuesday						
Wednesday						
Thursday						
Friday						
Saturday						
Sunday						
				Total Hours		
Notes:						

Name:	Month/Year:

Day	Date	Time in	Time out	Breaks	Overtime	Total
Monday						
Tuesday						
Wednesday						
Thursday						
Friday						
Saturday						
Sunday						
				Total Hours		
Notes:						

Name:	Month/Year:

Day	Date	Time in	Time out	Breaks	Overtime	Total
Monday						
Tuesday						
Wednesday						
Thursday						
Friday						
Saturday						
Sunday						
				Total Hours		

Notes:

Name:	Month/Year:

Day	Date	Time in	Time out	Breaks	Overtime	Total
Monday						
Tuesday						
Wednesday						
Thursday						
Friday						
Saturday						
Sunday						
				Total Hours		

Notes:

Name:	Month/Year:

Day	Date	Time in	Time out	Breaks	Overtime	Total
Monday						
Tuesday						
Wednesday						
Thursday						
Friday						
Saturday						
Sunday						
				Total Hours		
Notes:						

Name:	Month/Year:

Day	Date	Time in	Time out	Breaks	Overtime	Total
Monday						
Tuesday						
Wednesday						
Thursday						
Friday						
Saturday						
Sunday						
				Total Hours		
Notes:						

Name:	Month/Year:

Day	Date	Time in	Time out	Breaks	Overtime	Total
Monday						
Tuesday						
Wednesday						
Thursday						
Friday						
Saturday						
Sunday						
				Total Hours		
Notes:						

Name:	Month/Year:

Day	Date	Time in	Time out	Breaks	Overtime	Total
Monday						
Tuesday						
Wednesday						
Thursday						
Friday						
Saturday						
Sunday						
				Total Hours		
Notes:						

Name:	Month/Year:

Day	Date	Time in	Time out	Breaks	Overtime	Total
Monday						
Tuesday						
Wednesday						
Thursday						
Friday						
Saturday						
Sunday						
				Total Hours		
Notes:						

Name:	Month/Year:

Day	Date	Time in	Time out	Breaks	Overtime	Total
Monday						
Tuesday						
Wednesday						
Thursday						
Friday						
Saturday						
Sunday						
				Total Hours		
Notes:						

Name:	Month/Year:

Day	Date	Time in	Time out	Breaks	Overtime	Total
Monday						
Tuesday						
Wednesday						
Thursday						
Friday						
Saturday						
Sunday						
				Total Hours		
Notes:						

Name:	Month/Year:

Day	Date	Time in	Time out	Breaks	Overtime	Total
Monday						
Tuesday						
Wednesday						
Thursday						
Friday						
Saturday						
Sunday						
				Total Hours		
Notes:						

Name:	Month/Year:

Day	Date	Time in	Time out	Breaks	Overtime	Total
Monday						
Tuesday						
Wednesday						
Thursday						
Friday						
Saturday						
Sunday						
				Total Hours		
Notes:						

Name:	Month/Year:

Day	Date	Time in	Time out	Breaks	Overtime	Total
Monday						
Tuesday						
Wednesday						
Thursday						
Friday						
Saturday						
Sunday						
				Total Hours		
Notes:						

Name:	Month/Year:

Day	Date	Time in	Time out	Breaks	Overtime	Total
Monday						
Tuesday						
Wednesday						
Thursday						
Friday						
Saturday						
Sunday						
				Total Hours		
Notes:						

Name:	Month/Year:

Day	Date	Time in	Time out	Breaks	Overtime	Total
Monday						
Tuesday						
Wednesday						
Thursday						
Friday						
Saturday						
Sunday						
				Total Hours		
Notes:						

Name:	Month/Year:

Day	Date	Time in	Time out	Breaks	Overtime	Total
Monday						
Tuesday						
Wednesday						
Thursday						
Friday						
Saturday						
Sunday						
				Total Hours		
Notes:						

Name:	Month/Year:

Day	Date	Time in	Time out	Breaks	Overtime	Total
Monday						
Tuesday						
Wednesday						
Thursday						
Friday						
Saturday						
Sunday						
				Total Hours		
Notes:						

Name:	Month/Year:

Day	Date	Time in	Time out	Breaks	Overtime	Total
Monday						
Tuesday						
Wednesday						
Thursday						
Friday						
Saturday						
Sunday						
				Total Hours		
Notes:						

Name:	Month/Year:

Day	Date	Time in	Time out	Breaks	Overtime	Total
Monday						
Tuesday						
Wednesday						
Thursday						
Friday						
Saturday						
Sunday						
				Total Hours		
Notes:						

Name:	Month/Year:

Day	Date	Time in	Time out	Breaks	Overtime	Total
Monday						
Tuesday						
Wednesday						
Thursday						
Friday						
Saturday						
Sunday						
				Total Hours		
Notes:						

Name:	Month/Year:

Day	Date	Time in	Time out	Breaks	Overtime	Total
Monday						
Tuesday						
Wednesday						
Thursday						
Friday						
Saturday						
Sunday						
				Total Hours		
Notes:						

Name:	Month/Year:

Day	Date	Time in	Time out	Breaks	Overtime	Total
Monday						
Tuesday						
Wednesday						
Thursday						
Friday						
Saturday						
Sunday						
				Total Hours		
Notes:						

Name:	Month/Year:

Day	Date	Time in	Time out	Breaks	Overtime	Total
Monday						
Tuesday						
Wednesday						
Thursday						
Friday						
Saturday						
Sunday						
				Total Hours		
Notes:						

Name:	Month/Year:

Day	Date	Time in	Time out	Breaks	Overtime	Total
Monday						
Tuesday						
Wednesday						
Thursday						
Friday						
Saturday						
Sunday						
				Total Hours		

Notes:

Name:	Month/Year:

Day	Date	Time in	Time out	Breaks	Overtime	Total
Monday						
Tuesday						
Wednesday						
Thursday						
Friday						
Saturday						
Sunday						
				Total Hours		

Notes:

Name:	Month/Year:

Day	Date	Time in	Time out	Breaks	Overtime	Total
Monday						
Tuesday						
Wednesday						
Thursday						
Friday						
Saturday						
Sunday						
				Total Hours		
Notes:						

Name:	Month/Year:

Day	Date	Time in	Time out	Breaks	Overtime	Total
Monday						
Tuesday						
Wednesday						
Thursday						
Friday						
Saturday						
Sunday						
				Total Hours		
Notes:						

Name:	Month/Year:

Day	Date	Time in	Time out	Breaks	Overtime	Total
Monday						
Tuesday						
Wednesday						
Thursday						
Friday						
Saturday						
Sunday						
				Total Hours		
Notes:						

Name:	Month/Year:

Day	Date	Time in	Time out	Breaks	Overtime	Total
Monday						
Tuesday						
Wednesday						
Thursday						
Friday						
Saturday						
Sunday						
				Total Hours		
Notes:						

Name:	Month/Year:

Day	Date	Time in	Time out	Breaks	Overtime	Total
Monday						
Tuesday						
Wednesday						
Thursday						
Friday						
Saturday						
Sunday						
				Total Hours		
Notes:						

Name:	Month/Year:

Day	Date	Time in	Time out	Breaks	Overtime	Total
Monday						
Tuesday						
Wednesday						
Thursday						
Friday						
Saturday						
Sunday						
				Total Hours		
Notes:						

Name:	Month/Year:

Day	Date	Time in	Time out	Breaks	Overtime	Total
Monday						
Tuesday						
Wednesday						
Thursday						
Friday						
Saturday						
Sunday						
				Total Hours		
Notes:						

Name:	Month/Year:

Day	Date	Time in	Time out	Breaks	Overtime	Total
Monday						
Tuesday						
Wednesday						
Thursday						
Friday						
Saturday						
Sunday						
				Total Hours		
Notes:						

Name:	Month/Year:

Day	Date	Time in	Time out	Breaks	Overtime	Total
Monday						
Tuesday						
Wednesday						
Thursday						
Friday						
Saturday						
Sunday						
				Total Hours		
Notes:						

Name:	Month/Year:

Day	Date	Time in	Time out	Breaks	Overtime	Total
Monday						
Tuesday						
Wednesday						
Thursday						
Friday						
Saturday						
Sunday						
				Total Hours		
Notes:						

Name:	Month/Year:

Day	Date	Time in	Time out	Breaks	Overtime	Total
Monday						
Tuesday						
Wednesday						
Thursday						
Friday						
Saturday						
Sunday						
				Total Hours		
Notes:						

Name:	Month/Year:

Day	Date	Time in	Time out	Breaks	Overtime	Total
Monday						
Tuesday						
Wednesday						
Thursday						
Friday						
Saturday						
Sunday						
				Total Hours		
Notes:						

Name:	Month/Year:

Day	Date	Time in	Time out	Breaks	Overtime	Total
Monday						
Tuesday						
Wednesday						
Thursday						
Friday						
Saturday						
Sunday						
				Total Hours		
Notes:						

Name:	Month/Year:

Day	Date	Time in	Time out	Breaks	Overtime	Total
Monday						
Tuesday						
Wednesday						
Thursday						
Friday						
Saturday						
Sunday						
				Total Hours		
Notes:						

Name:	Month/Year:

Day	Date	Time in	Time out	Breaks	Overtime	Total
Monday						
Tuesday						
Wednesday						
Thursday						
Friday						
Saturday						
Sunday						
				Total Hours		

Notes:

Name:	Month/Year:

Day	Date	Time in	Time out	Breaks	Overtime	Total
Monday						
Tuesday						
Wednesday						
Thursday						
Friday						
Saturday						
Sunday						
				Total Hours		

Notes:

Name:	Month/Year:

Day	Date	Time in	Time out	Breaks	Overtime	Total
Monday						
Tuesday						
Wednesday						
Thursday						
Friday						
Saturday						
Sunday						
				Total Hours		
Notes:						

Name:	Month/Year:

Day	Date	Time in	Time out	Breaks	Overtime	Total
Monday						
Tuesday						
Wednesday						
Thursday						
Friday						
Saturday						
Sunday						
				Total Hours		
Notes:						

Name:	Month/Year:

Day	Date	Time in	Time out	Breaks	Overtime	Total
Monday						
Tuesday						
Wednesday						
Thursday						
Friday						
Saturday						
Sunday						
				Total Hours		
Notes:						

Name:	Month/Year:

Day	Date	Time in	Time out	Breaks	Overtime	Total
Monday						
Tuesday						
Wednesday						
Thursday						
Friday						
Saturday						
Sunday						
				Total Hours		
Notes:						

Name:	Month/Year:

Day	Date	Time in	Time out	Breaks	Overtime	Total
Monday						
Tuesday						
Wednesday						
Thursday						
Friday						
Saturday						
Sunday						
				Total Hours		

Notes:

Name:	Month/Year:

Day	Date	Time in	Time out	Breaks	Overtime	Total
Monday						
Tuesday						
Wednesday						
Thursday						
Friday						
Saturday						
Sunday						
				Total Hours		

Notes:

Name:	Month/Year:

Day	Date	Time in	Time out	Breaks	Overtime	Total
Monday						
Tuesday						
Wednesday						
Thursday						
Friday						
Saturday						
Sunday						
				Total Hours		
Notes:						

Name:	Month/Year:

Day	Date	Time in	Time out	Breaks	Overtime	Total
Monday						
Tuesday						
Wednesday						
Thursday						
Friday						
Saturday						
Sunday						
				Total Hours		
Notes:						

Name:	Month/Year:

Day	Date	Time in	Time out	Breaks	Overtime	Total
Monday						
Tuesday						
Wednesday						
Thursday						
Friday						
Saturday						
Sunday						
				Total Hours		
Notes:						

Name:	Month/Year:

Day	Date	Time in	Time out	Breaks	Overtime	Total
Monday						
Tuesday						
Wednesday						
Thursday						
Friday						
Saturday						
Sunday						
				Total Hours		
Notes:						

Name:	Month/Year:

Day	Date	Time in	Time out	Breaks	Overtime	Total
Monday						
Tuesday						
Wednesday						
Thursday						
Friday						
Saturday						
Sunday						
				Total Hours		
Notes:						

Name:	Month/Year:

Day	Date	Time in	Time out	Breaks	Overtime	Total
Monday						
Tuesday						
Wednesday						
Thursday						
Friday						
Saturday						
Sunday						
				Total Hours		
Notes:						

Name:	Month/Year:

Day	Date	Time in	Time out	Breaks	Overtime	Total
Monday						
Tuesday						
Wednesday						
Thursday						
Friday						
Saturday						
Sunday						
				Total Hours		
Notes:						

Name:	Month/Year:

Day	Date	Time in	Time out	Breaks	Overtime	Total
Monday						
Tuesday						
Wednesday						
Thursday						
Friday						
Saturday						
Sunday						
				Total Hours		
Notes:						

Name:	Month/Year:

Day	Date	Time in	Time out	Breaks	Overtime	Total
Monday						
Tuesday						
Wednesday						
Thursday						
Friday						
Saturday						
Sunday						
				Total Hours		
Notes:						

Name:	Month/Year:

Day	Date	Time in	Time out	Breaks	Overtime	Total
Monday						
Tuesday						
Wednesday						
Thursday						
Friday						
Saturday						
Sunday						
				Total Hours		
Notes:						

Name:	Month/Year:

Day	Date	Time in	Time out	Breaks	Overtime	Total
Monday						
Tuesday						
Wednesday						
Thursday						
Friday						
Saturday						
Sunday						
				Total Hours		
Notes:						

Name:	Month/Year:

Day	Date	Time in	Time out	Breaks	Overtime	Total
Monday						
Tuesday						
Wednesday						
Thursday						
Friday						
Saturday						
Sunday						
				Total Hours		
Notes:						

Name:	Month/Year:

Day	Date	Time in	Time out	Breaks	Overtime	Total
Monday						
Tuesday						
Wednesday						
Thursday						
Friday						
Saturday						
Sunday						
				Total Hours		
Notes:						

Name:	Month/Year:

Day	Date	Time in	Time out	Breaks	Overtime	Total
Monday						
Tuesday						
Wednesday						
Thursday						
Friday						
Saturday						
Sunday						
				Total Hours		
Notes:						

Name:	Month/Year:

Day	Date	Time in	Time out	Breaks	Overtime	Total
Monday						
Tuesday						
Wednesday						
Thursday						
Friday						
Saturday						
Sunday						
				Total Hours		
Notes:						

Name:	Month/Year:

Day	Date	Time in	Time out	Breaks	Overtime	Total
Monday						
Tuesday						
Wednesday						
Thursday						
Friday						
Saturday						
Sunday						
				Total Hours		
Notes:						

Name:	Month/Year:

Day	Date	Time in	Time out	Breaks	Overtime	Total
Monday						
Tuesday						
Wednesday						
Thursday						
Friday						
Saturday						
Sunday						
				Total Hours		
Notes:						

Name:	Month/Year:

Day	Date	Time in	Time out	Breaks	Overtime	Total
Monday						
Tuesday						
Wednesday						
Thursday						
Friday						
Saturday						
Sunday						
				Total Hours		
Notes:						

Name:	Month/Year:

Day	Date	Time in	Time out	Breaks	Overtime	Total
Monday						
Tuesday						
Wednesday						
Thursday						
Friday						
Saturday						
Sunday						
				Total Hours		
Notes:						

Name:	Month/Year:

Day	Date	Time in	Time out	Breaks	Overtime	Total
Monday						
Tuesday						
Wednesday						
Thursday						
Friday						
Saturday						
Sunday						
				Total Hours		
Notes:						

Name:	Month/Year:

Day	Date	Time in	Time out	Breaks	Overtime	Total
Monday						
Tuesday						
Wednesday						
Thursday						
Friday						
Saturday						
Sunday						
				Total Hours		

Notes:

Name:	Month/Year:

Day	Date	Time in	Time out	Breaks	Overtime	Total
Monday						
Tuesday						
Wednesday						
Thursday						
Friday						
Saturday						
Sunday						
				Total Hours		

Notes:

Name:	Month/Year:

Day	Date	Time in	Time out	Breaks	Overtime	Total
Monday						
Tuesday						
Wednesday						
Thursday						
Friday						
Saturday						
Sunday						
				Total Hours		

Notes:

Name:	Month/Year:

Day	Date	Time in	Time out	Breaks	Overtime	Total
Monday						
Tuesday						
Wednesday						
Thursday						
Friday						
Saturday						
Sunday						
				Total Hours		

Notes:

Name:	Month/Year:

Day	Date	Time in	Time out	Breaks	Overtime	Total
Monday						
Tuesday						
Wednesday						
Thursday						
Friday						
Saturday						
Sunday						
				Total Hours		
Notes:						

Name:	Month/Year:

Day	Date	Time in	Time out	Breaks	Overtime	Total
Monday						
Tuesday						
Wednesday						
Thursday						
Friday						
Saturday						
Sunday						
				Total Hours		
Notes:						

Name:	Month/Year:

Day	Date	Time in	Time out	Breaks	Overtime	Total
Monday						
Tuesday						
Wednesday						
Thursday						
Friday						
Saturday						
Sunday						
				Total Hours		
Notes:						

Name:	Month/Year:

Day	Date	Time in	Time out	Breaks	Overtime	Total
Monday						
Tuesday						
Wednesday						
Thursday						
Friday						
Saturday						
Sunday						
				Total Hours		
Notes:						

Name:	Month/Year:

Day	Date	Time in	Time out	Breaks	Overtime	Total
Monday						
Tuesday						
Wednesday						
Thursday						
Friday						
Saturday						
Sunday						
				Total Hours		

Notes:

Name:	Month/Year:

Day	Date	Time in	Time out	Breaks	Overtime	Total
Monday						
Tuesday						
Wednesday						
Thursday						
Friday						
Saturday						
Sunday						
				Total Hours		

Notes:

Name:	Month/Year:

Day	Date	Time in	Time out	Breaks	Overtime	Total
Monday						
Tuesday						
Wednesday						
Thursday						
Friday						
Saturday						
Sunday						
				Total Hours		
Notes:						

Name:	Month/Year:

Day	Date	Time in	Time out	Breaks	Overtime	Total
Monday						
Tuesday						
Wednesday						
Thursday						
Friday						
Saturday						
Sunday						
				Total Hours		
Notes:						

Name:	Month/Year:

Day	Date	Time in	Time out	Breaks	Overtime	Total
Monday						
Tuesday						
Wednesday						
Thursday						
Friday						
Saturday						
Sunday						
				Total Hours		
Notes:						

Name:	Month/Year:

Day	Date	Time in	Time out	Breaks	Overtime	Total
Monday						
Tuesday						
Wednesday						
Thursday						
Friday						
Saturday						
Sunday						
				Total Hours		
Notes:						

Name:	Month/Year:

Day	Date	Time in	Time out	Breaks	Overtime	Total
Monday						
Tuesday						
Wednesday						
Thursday						
Friday						
Saturday						
Sunday						
				Total Hours		

Notes:

Name:	Month/Year:

Day	Date	Time in	Time out	Breaks	Overtime	Total
Monday						
Tuesday						
Wednesday						
Thursday						
Friday						
Saturday						
Sunday						
				Total Hours		

Notes:

Name:	Month/Year:

Day	Date	Time in	Time out	Breaks	Overtime	Total
Monday						
Tuesday						
Wednesday						
Thursday						
Friday						
Saturday						
Sunday						
				Total Hours		
Notes:						

Name:	Month/Year:

Day	Date	Time in	Time out	Breaks	Overtime	Total
Monday						
Tuesday						
Wednesday						
Thursday						
Friday						
Saturday						
Sunday						
				Total Hours		
Notes:						

Name:	Month/Year:

Day	Date	Time in	Time out	Breaks	Overtime	Total
Monday						
Tuesday						
Wednesday						
Thursday						
Friday						
Saturday						
Sunday						
				Total Hours		

Notes:

Name:	Month/Year:

Day	Date	Time in	Time out	Breaks	Overtime	Total
Monday						
Tuesday						
Wednesday						
Thursday						
Friday						
Saturday						
Sunday						
				Total Hours		

Notes:

Name:	Month/Year:

Day	Date	Time in	Time out	Breaks	Overtime	Total
Monday						
Tuesday						
Wednesday						
Thursday						
Friday						
Saturday						
Sunday						
				Total Hours		
Notes:						

Name:	Month/Year:

Day	Date	Time in	Time out	Breaks	Overtime	Total
Monday						
Tuesday						
Wednesday						
Thursday						
Friday						
Saturday						
Sunday						
				Total Hours		
Notes:						

Name:	Month/Year:

Day	Date	Time in	Time out	Breaks	Overtime	Total
Monday						
Tuesday						
Wednesday						
Thursday						
Friday						
Saturday						
Sunday						
				Total Hours		

Notes:

Name:	Month/Year:

Day	Date	Time in	Time out	Breaks	Overtime	Total
Monday						
Tuesday						
Wednesday						
Thursday						
Friday						
Saturday						
Sunday						
				Total Hours		

Notes:

Name:	Month/Year:

Day	Date	Time in	Time out	Breaks	Overtime	Total
Monday						
Tuesday						
Wednesday						
Thursday						
Friday						
Saturday						
Sunday						
				Total Hours		
Notes:						

Name:	Month/Year:

Day	Date	Time in	Time out	Breaks	Overtime	Total
Monday						
Tuesday						
Wednesday						
Thursday						
Friday						
Saturday						
Sunday						
				Total Hours		
Notes:						

Name:	Month/Year:

Day	Date	Time in	Time out	Breaks	Overtime	Total
Monday						
Tuesday						
Wednesday						
Thursday						
Friday						
Saturday						
Sunday						
				Total Hours		

Notes:

Name:	Month/Year:

Day	Date	Time in	Time out	Breaks	Overtime	Total
Monday						
Tuesday						
Wednesday						
Thursday						
Friday						
Saturday						
Sunday						
				Total Hours		

Notes:

Name:	Month/Year:

Day	Date	Time in	Time out	Breaks	Overtime	Total
Monday						
Tuesday						
Wednesday						
Thursday						
Friday						
Saturday						
Sunday						
				Total Hours		
Notes:						

Name:	Month/Year:

Day	Date	Time in	Time out	Breaks	Overtime	Total
Monday						
Tuesday						
Wednesday						
Thursday						
Friday						
Saturday						
Sunday						
				Total Hours		
Notes:						

Name:	Month/Year:

Day	Date	Time in	Time out	Breaks	Overtime	Total
Monday						
Tuesday						
Wednesday						
Thursday						
Friday						
Saturday						
Sunday						
				Total Hours		
Notes:						

Name:	Month/Year:

Day	Date	Time in	Time out	Breaks	Overtime	Total
Monday						
Tuesday						
Wednesday						
Thursday						
Friday						
Saturday						
Sunday						
				Total Hours		
Notes:						

Name:	Month/Year:

Day	Date	Time in	Time out	Breaks	Overtime	Total
Monday						
Tuesday						
Wednesday						
Thursday						
Friday						
Saturday						
Sunday						
				Total Hours		
Notes:						

Name:	Month/Year:

Day	Date	Time in	Time out	Breaks	Overtime	Total
Monday						
Tuesday						
Wednesday						
Thursday						
Friday						
Saturday						
Sunday						
				Total Hours		
Notes:						

Name:	Month/Year:

Day	Date	Time in	Time out	Breaks	Overtime	Total
Monday						
Tuesday						
Wednesday						
Thursday						
Friday						
Saturday						
Sunday						
				Total Hours		

Notes:

Name:	Month/Year:

Day	Date	Time in	Time out	Breaks	Overtime	Total
Monday						
Tuesday						
Wednesday						
Thursday						
Friday						
Saturday						
Sunday						
				Total Hours		

Notes:

Name:	Month/Year:

Day	Date	Time in	Time out	Breaks	Overtime	Total
Monday						
Tuesday						
Wednesday						
Thursday						
Friday						
Saturday						
Sunday						
				Total Hours		
Notes:						

Name:	Month/Year:

Day	Date	Time in	Time out	Breaks	Overtime	Total
Monday						
Tuesday						
Wednesday						
Thursday						
Friday						
Saturday						
Sunday						
				Total Hours		
Notes:						

Name:	Month/Year:

Day	Date	Time in	Time out	Breaks	Overtime	Total
Monday						
Tuesday						
Wednesday						
Thursday						
Friday						
Saturday						
Sunday						
				Total Hours		
Notes:						

Name:	Month/Year:

Day	Date	Time in	Time out	Breaks	Overtime	Total
Monday						
Tuesday						
Wednesday						
Thursday						
Friday						
Saturday						
Sunday						
				Total Hours		
Notes:						

Name:	Month/Year:

Day	Date	Time in	Time out	Breaks	Overtime	Total
Monday						
Tuesday						
Wednesday						
Thursday						
Friday						
Saturday						
Sunday						
				Total Hours		
Notes:						

Name:	Month/Year:

Day	Date	Time in	Time out	Breaks	Overtime	Total
Monday						
Tuesday						
Wednesday						
Thursday						
Friday						
Saturday						
Sunday						
				Total Hours		
Notes:						

Name:	Month/Year:

Day	Date	Time in	Time out	Breaks	Overtime	Total
Monday						
Tuesday						
Wednesday						
Thursday						
Friday						
Saturday						
Sunday						
				Total Hours		
Notes:						

Name:	Month/Year:

Day	Date	Time in	Time out	Breaks	Overtime	Total
Monday						
Tuesday						
Wednesday						
Thursday						
Friday						
Saturday						
Sunday						
				Total Hours		
Notes:						

Name:	Month/Year:

Day	Date	Time in	Time out	Breaks	Overtime	Total
Monday						
Tuesday						
Wednesday						
Thursday						
Friday						
Saturday						
Sunday						
				Total Hours		
Notes:						

Name:	Month/Year:

Day	Date	Time in	Time out	Breaks	Overtime	Total
Monday						
Tuesday						
Wednesday						
Thursday						
Friday						
Saturday						
Sunday						
				Total Hours		
Notes:						

Name:	Month/Year:

Day	Date	Time in	Time out	Breaks	Overtime	Total
Monday						
Tuesday						
Wednesday						
Thursday						
Friday						
Saturday						
Sunday						
				Total Hours		
Notes:						

Name:	Month/Year:

Day	Date	Time in	Time out	Breaks	Overtime	Total
Monday						
Tuesday						
Wednesday						
Thursday						
Friday						
Saturday						
Sunday						
				Total Hours		
Notes:						

Name:	Month/Year:

Day	Date	Time in	Time out	Breaks	Overtime	Total
Monday						
Tuesday						
Wednesday						
Thursday						
Friday						
Saturday						
Sunday						
				Total Hours		

Notes:

Name:	Month/Year:

Day	Date	Time in	Time out	Breaks	Overtime	Total
Monday						
Tuesday						
Wednesday						
Thursday						
Friday						
Saturday						
Sunday						
				Total Hours		

Notes:

Name:	Month/Year:

Day	Date	Time in	Time out	Breaks	Overtime	Total
Monday						
Tuesday						
Wednesday						
Thursday						
Friday						
Saturday						
Sunday						
				Total Hours		

Notes:

Name:	Month/Year:

Day	Date	Time in	Time out	Breaks	Overtime	Total
Monday						
Tuesday						
Wednesday						
Thursday						
Friday						
Saturday						
Sunday						
				Total Hours		

Notes:

Name:	Month/Year:

Day	Date	Time in	Time out	Breaks	Overtime	Total
Monday						
Tuesday						
Wednesday						
Thursday						
Friday						
Saturday						
Sunday						
				Total Hours		
Notes:						

Name:	Month/Year:

Day	Date	Time in	Time out	Breaks	Overtime	Total
Monday						
Tuesday						
Wednesday						
Thursday						
Friday						
Saturday						
Sunday						
				Total Hours		
Notes:						

Name:	Month/Year:

Day	Date	Time in	Time out	Breaks	Overtime	Total
Monday						
Tuesday						
Wednesday						
Thursday						
Friday						
Saturday						
Sunday						
				Total Hours		

Notes:

Name:	Month/Year:

Day	Date	Time in	Time out	Breaks	Overtime	Total
Monday						
Tuesday						
Wednesday						
Thursday						
Friday						
Saturday						
Sunday						
				Total Hours		

Notes:

Name:	Month/Year:

Day	Date	Time in	Time out	Breaks	Overtime	Total
Monday						
Tuesday						
Wednesday						
Thursday						
Friday						
Saturday						
Sunday						
				Total Hours		
Notes:						

Name:	Month/Year:

Day	Date	Time in	Time out	Breaks	Overtime	Total
Monday						
Tuesday						
Wednesday						
Thursday						
Friday						
Saturday						
Sunday						
				Total Hours		
Notes:						

Name:	Month/Year:

Day	Date	Time in	Time out	Breaks	Overtime	Total
Monday						
Tuesday						
Wednesday						
Thursday						
Friday						
Saturday						
Sunday						
				Total Hours		
Notes:						

Name:	Month/Year:

Day	Date	Time in	Time out	Breaks	Overtime	Total
Monday						
Tuesday						
Wednesday						
Thursday						
Friday						
Saturday						
Sunday						
				Total Hours		
Notes:						

Name:	Month/Year:

Day	Date	Time in	Time out	Breaks	Overtime	Total
Monday						
Tuesday						
Wednesday						
Thursday						
Friday						
Saturday						
Sunday						
				Total Hours		
Notes:						

Name:	Month/Year:

Day	Date	Time in	Time out	Breaks	Overtime	Total
Monday						
Tuesday						
Wednesday						
Thursday						
Friday						
Saturday						
Sunday						
				Total Hours		
Notes:						

Name:	Month/Year:

Day	Date	Time in	Time out	Breaks	Overtime	Total
Monday						
Tuesday						
Wednesday						
Thursday						
Friday						
Saturday						
Sunday						
				Total Hours		
Notes:						

Name:	Month/Year:

Day	Date	Time in	Time out	Breaks	Overtime	Total
Monday						
Tuesday						
Wednesday						
Thursday						
Friday						
Saturday						
Sunday						
				Total Hours		
Notes:						

Name:	Month/Year:

Day	Date	Time in	Time out	Breaks	Overtime	Total
Monday						
Tuesday						
Wednesday						
Thursday						
Friday						
Saturday						
Sunday						
				Total Hours		
Notes:						

Name:	Month/Year:

Day	Date	Time in	Time out	Breaks	Overtime	Total
Monday						
Tuesday						
Wednesday						
Thursday						
Friday						
Saturday						
Sunday						
				Total Hours		
Notes:						

Name:	Month/Year:

Day	Date	Time in	Time out	Breaks	Overtime	Total
Monday						
Tuesday						
Wednesday						
Thursday						
Friday						
Saturday						
Sunday						
				Total Hours		

Notes:

Name:	Month/Year:

Day	Date	Time in	Time out	Breaks	Overtime	Total
Monday						
Tuesday						
Wednesday						
Thursday						
Friday						
Saturday						
Sunday						
				Total Hours		

Notes:

Name:	Month/Year:

Day	Date	Time in	Time out	Breaks	Overtime	Total
Monday						
Tuesday						
Wednesday						
Thursday						
Friday						
Saturday						
Sunday						
				Total Hours		
Notes:						

Name:	Month/Year:

Day	Date	Time in	Time out	Breaks	Overtime	Total
Monday						
Tuesday						
Wednesday						
Thursday						
Friday						
Saturday						
Sunday						
				Total Hours		
Notes:						

Name:	Month/Year:

Day	Date	Time in	Time out	Breaks	Overtime	Total
Monday						
Tuesday						
Wednesday						
Thursday						
Friday						
Saturday						
Sunday						
				Total Hours		
Notes:						

Name:	Month/Year:

Day	Date	Time in	Time out	Breaks	Overtime	Total
Monday						
Tuesday						
Wednesday						
Thursday						
Friday						
Saturday						
Sunday						
				Total Hours		
Notes:						

Name:	Month/Year:

Day	Date	Time in	Time out	Breaks	Overtime	Total
Monday						
Tuesday						
Wednesday						
Thursday						
Friday						
Saturday						
Sunday						
				Total Hours		
Notes:						

Name:	Month/Year:

Day	Date	Time in	Time out	Breaks	Overtime	Total
Monday						
Tuesday						
Wednesday						
Thursday						
Friday						
Saturday						
Sunday						
				Total Hours		
Notes:						

Name:	Month/Year:

Day	Date	Time in	Time out	Breaks	Overtime	Total
Monday						
Tuesday						
Wednesday						
Thursday						
Friday						
Saturday						
Sunday						
				Total Hours		
Notes:						

Name:	Month/Year:

Day	Date	Time in	Time out	Breaks	Overtime	Total
Monday						
Tuesday						
Wednesday						
Thursday						
Friday						
Saturday						
Sunday						
				Total Hours		
Notes:						

Name:	Month/Year:

Day	Date	Time in	Time out	Breaks	Overtime	Total
Monday						
Tuesday						
Wednesday						
Thursday						
Friday						
Saturday						
Sunday						
				Total Hours		
Notes:						

Name:	Month/Year:

Day	Date	Time in	Time out	Breaks	Overtime	Total
Monday						
Tuesday						
Wednesday						
Thursday						
Friday						
Saturday						
Sunday						
				Total Hours		
Notes:						

Name:	Month/Year:

Day	Date	Time in	Time out	Breaks	Overtime	Total
Monday						
Tuesday						
Wednesday						
Thursday						
Friday						
Saturday						
Sunday						
				Total Hours		

Notes:

Name:	Month/Year:

Day	Date	Time in	Time out	Breaks	Overtime	Total
Monday						
Tuesday						
Wednesday						
Thursday						
Friday						
Saturday						
Sunday						
				Total Hours		

Notes:

Name:	Month/Year:

Day	Date	Time in	Time out	Breaks	Overtime	Total
Monday						
Tuesday						
Wednesday						
Thursday						
Friday						
Saturday						
Sunday						
				Total Hours		
Notes:						

Name:	Month/Year:

Day	Date	Time in	Time out	Breaks	Overtime	Total
Monday						
Tuesday						
Wednesday						
Thursday						
Friday						
Saturday						
Sunday						
				Total Hours		
Notes:						

Name:	Month/Year:

Day	Date	Time in	Time out	Breaks	Overtime	Total
Monday						
Tuesday						
Wednesday						
Thursday						
Friday						
Saturday						
Sunday						
				Total Hours		
Notes:						

Name:	Month/Year:

Day	Date	Time in	Time out	Breaks	Overtime	Total
Monday						
Tuesday						
Wednesday						
Thursday						
Friday						
Saturday						
Sunday						
				Total Hours		
Notes:						

Name:	Month/Year:

Day	Date	Time in	Time out	Breaks	Overtime	Total
Monday						
Tuesday						
Wednesday						
Thursday						
Friday						
Saturday						
Sunday						
				Total Hours		

Notes:

Name:	Month/Year:

Day	Date	Time in	Time out	Breaks	Overtime	Total
Monday						
Tuesday						
Wednesday						
Thursday						
Friday						
Saturday						
Sunday						
				Total Hours		

Notes:

Name:	Month/Year:

Day	Date	Time in	Time out	Breaks	Overtime	Total
Monday						
Tuesday						
Wednesday						
Thursday						
Friday						
Saturday						
Sunday						
				Total Hours		
Notes:						

Name:	Month/Year:

Day	Date	Time in	Time out	Breaks	Overtime	Total
Monday						
Tuesday						
Wednesday						
Thursday						
Friday						
Saturday						
Sunday						
				Total Hours		
Notes:						

Name:	Month/Year:

Day	Date	Time in	Time out	Breaks	Overtime	Total
Monday						
Tuesday						
Wednesday						
Thursday						
Friday						
Saturday						
Sunday						
				Total Hours		

Notes:

Name:	Month/Year:

Day	Date	Time in	Time out	Breaks	Overtime	Total
Monday						
Tuesday						
Wednesday						
Thursday						
Friday						
Saturday						
Sunday						
				Total Hours		

Notes:

Name:	Month/Year:

Day	Date	Time in	Time out	Breaks	Overtime	Total
Monday						
Tuesday						
Wednesday						
Thursday						
Friday						
Saturday						
Sunday						
				Total Hours		
Notes:						

Name:	Month/Year:

Day	Date	Time in	Time out	Breaks	Overtime	Total
Monday						
Tuesday						
Wednesday						
Thursday						
Friday						
Saturday						
Sunday						
				Total Hours		
Notes:						

Name:	Month/Year:

Day	Date	Time in	Time out	Breaks	Overtime	Total
Monday						
Tuesday						
Wednesday						
Thursday						
Friday						
Saturday						
Sunday						
				Total Hours		
Notes:						

Name:	Month/Year:

Day	Date	Time in	Time out	Breaks	Overtime	Total
Monday						
Tuesday						
Wednesday						
Thursday						
Friday						
Saturday						
Sunday						
				Total Hours		
Notes:						

Name:	Month/Year:

Day	Date	Time in	Time out	Breaks	Overtime	Total
Monday						
Tuesday						
Wednesday						
Thursday						
Friday						
Saturday						
Sunday						
				Total Hours		
Notes:						

Name:	Month/Year:

Day	Date	Time in	Time out	Breaks	Overtime	Total
Monday						
Tuesday						
Wednesday						
Thursday						
Friday						
Saturday						
Sunday						
				Total Hours		
Notes:						

Name:	Month/Year:

Day	Date	Time in	Time out	Breaks	Overtime	Total
Monday						
Tuesday						
Wednesday						
Thursday						
Friday						
Saturday						
Sunday						
				Total Hours		
Notes:						

Name:	Month/Year:

Day	Date	Time in	Time out	Breaks	Overtime	Total
Monday						
Tuesday						
Wednesday						
Thursday						
Friday						
Saturday						
Sunday						
				Total Hours		
Notes:						

Name:	Month/Year:

Day	Date	Time in	Time out	Breaks	Overtime	Total
Monday						
Tuesday						
Wednesday						
Thursday						
Friday						
Saturday						
Sunday						
				Total Hours		
Notes:						

Name:	Month/Year:

Day	Date	Time in	Time out	Breaks	Overtime	Total
Monday						
Tuesday						
Wednesday						
Thursday						
Friday						
Saturday						
Sunday						
				Total Hours		
Notes:						

Name:	Month/Year:

Day	Date	Time in	Time out	Breaks	Overtime	Total
Monday						
Tuesday						
Wednesday						
Thursday						
Friday						
Saturday						
Sunday						
				Total Hours		
Notes:						

Name:	Month/Year:

Day	Date	Time in	Time out	Breaks	Overtime	Total
Monday						
Tuesday						
Wednesday						
Thursday						
Friday						
Saturday						
Sunday						
				Total Hours		
Notes:						

Name:	Month/Year:

Day	Date	Time in	Time out	Breaks	Overtime	Total
Monday						
Tuesday						
Wednesday						
Thursday						
Friday						
Saturday						
Sunday						
				Total Hours		
Notes:						

Name:	Month/Year:

Day	Date	Time in	Time out	Breaks	Overtime	Total
Monday						
Tuesday						
Wednesday						
Thursday						
Friday						
Saturday						
Sunday						
				Total Hours		
Notes:						

Name:	Month/Year:

Day	Date	Time in	Time out	Breaks	Overtime	Total
Monday						
Tuesday						
Wednesday						
Thursday						
Friday						
Saturday						
Sunday						
				Total Hours		
Notes:						

Name:	Month/Year:

Day	Date	Time in	Time out	Breaks	Overtime	Total
Monday						
Tuesday						
Wednesday						
Thursday						
Friday						
Saturday						
Sunday						
				Total Hours		
Notes:						

Name:	Month/Year:

Day	Date	Time in	Time out	Breaks	Overtime	Total
Monday						
Tuesday						
Wednesday						
Thursday						
Friday						
Saturday						
Sunday						
				Total Hours		
Notes:						

Name:	Month/Year:

Day	Date	Time in	Time out	Breaks	Overtime	Total
Monday						
Tuesday						
Wednesday						
Thursday						
Friday						
Saturday						
Sunday						
				Total Hours		
Notes:						

Name:	Month/Year:

Day	Date	Time in	Time out	Breaks	Overtime	Total
Monday						
Tuesday						
Wednesday						
Thursday						
Friday						
Saturday						
Sunday						
				Total Hours		
Notes:						

Name:	Month/Year:

Day	Date	Time in	Time out	Breaks	Overtime	Total
Monday						
Tuesday						
Wednesday						
Thursday						
Friday						
Saturday						
Sunday						
				Total Hours		
Notes:						

Name:	Month/Year:

Day	Date	Time in	Time out	Breaks	Overtime	Total
Monday						
Tuesday						
Wednesday						
Thursday						
Friday						
Saturday						
Sunday						
				Total Hours		

Notes:

Name:	Month/Year:

Day	Date	Time in	Time out	Breaks	Overtime	Total
Monday						
Tuesday						
Wednesday						
Thursday						
Friday						
Saturday						
Sunday						
				Total Hours		

Notes:

Name:	Month/Year:

Day	Date	Time in	Time out	Breaks	Overtime	Total
Monday						
Tuesday						
Wednesday						
Thursday						
Friday						
Saturday						
Sunday						
				Total Hours		
Notes:						

Name:	Month/Year:

Day	Date	Time in	Time out	Breaks	Overtime	Total
Monday						
Tuesday						
Wednesday						
Thursday						
Friday						
Saturday						
Sunday						
				Total Hours		
Notes:						

Name:	Month/Year:

Day	Date	Time in	Time out	Breaks	Overtime	Total
Monday						
Tuesday						
Wednesday						
Thursday						
Friday						
Saturday						
Sunday						
				Total Hours		
Notes:						

Name:	Month/Year:

Day	Date	Time in	Time out	Breaks	Overtime	Total
Monday						
Tuesday						
Wednesday						
Thursday						
Friday						
Saturday						
Sunday						
				Total Hours		
Notes:						

Name:	Month/Year:

Day	Date	Time in	Time out	Breaks	Overtime	Total
Monday						
Tuesday						
Wednesday						
Thursday						
Friday						
Saturday						
Sunday						
				Total Hours		
Notes:						

Name:	Month/Year:

Day	Date	Time in	Time out	Breaks	Overtime	Total
Monday						
Tuesday						
Wednesday						
Thursday						
Friday						
Saturday						
Sunday						
				Total Hours		
Notes:						

Name:	Month/Year:

Day	Date	Time in	Time out	Breaks	Overtime	Total
Monday						
Tuesday						
Wednesday						
Thursday						
Friday						
Saturday						
Sunday						
				Total Hours		
Notes:						

Name:	Month/Year:

Day	Date	Time in	Time out	Breaks	Overtime	Total
Monday						
Tuesday						
Wednesday						
Thursday						
Friday						
Saturday						
Sunday						
				Total Hours		
Notes:						

Thank you!

WE ARE GLAD THAT YOU PURCHASED OUR BOOK!
PLEASE LET US KNOW HOW WE CAN IMPROVE IT!
YOUR FEEDBACK IS ESSENTIAL TO US.

Contact us at:

log'Sin@gmail.com

JUST TITLE THE EMAIL 'CREATIVE' AND WE WILL GIVE YOU SOME EXTRA SURPRISES!

CPSIA information can be obtained
at www.ICGtesting.com
Printed in the USA
LVHW061948191222
735554LV00011B/407